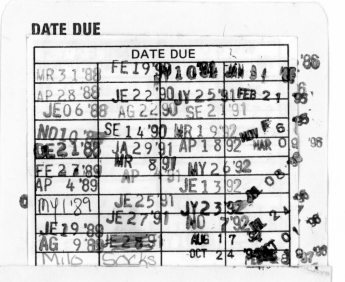

CATS

by Cynthia Overbeck

Photographs by Shin Yoshino

A Lerner Natural Science Book

Lerner Publications Company ▪ Minneapolis

Sylvia A. Johnson, Series Editor

Translation of original text by Kay Kushino

Additional photographs by: pp. 3, 15, 19, 26 (bottom), 27, 29, 35 (bottom), Klaus Paysan; pp. 5 (bottom), 11, 12, 16, 20, Tokumitsu Iwago

The glossary on page 46 gives definitions and pronunciations of words shown in **bold type** in the text.

To Norton and Alice, my two favorite tabbies

LIBRARY OF CONGRESS CATALOGING IN PUBLICATION DATA

Overbeck, Cynthia.
  Cats.

    (A Lerner natural science book)
    Adaptation of: Neko no kurashi / by Shin Yoshino.
    Includes index.
    Summary: Discusses the physical characteristics, birth, habits, and behavior of cats.
    1. Cats—Juvenile literature. [1. Cats]
I. Yoshino, Shin, 1943-   ill. II. Yoshino, Shin, 1943-   . Neko no kurashi. III. Title. IV. Series.

SF445.7.O94 1983   636.8   83-17530
ISBN 0-8225-1480-X (lib. bdg.)

This edition first published 1983 by Lerner Publications Company.
Text copyright © 1983 by Lerner Publications Company.
Photographs copyright © 1980 by Shin Yoshino.
Text adapted from CATS copyright © 1980 by Shin Yoshino.
English language rights arranged by Kurita-Bando Literary Agency for Akane Shobo Publishers, Tokyo, Japan.

International Standard Book Number: 0-8225-1480-X
Library of Congress Catalog Card Number: 83-17530

1 2 3 4 5 6 7 8 9 10 91 90 89 88 87 86 85 84 83

If you have a pet cat, you know how unpredictable it can be. One minute, it is rolling on its back, asking you to pet it. The next minute, it gets up and strolls away, ignoring you completely. On some days, your cat may be a charming, playful companion. On other days, it turns into a hunter, muscles tense and eyes alert.

In fact, your pet cat does have a kind of double identity. For centuries cats have been companions to human beings, yet they have not forgotten the ways of their wild ancestors.

All cats belong to the scientific family Felidae, which is divided into three main groups. The first group, *Panthera,* is made up of the big wild cats of Africa, Asia, and the Americas—lions, tigers, leopards, and jaguars. The second group, *Acinonyx,* consists only of cheetahs. The third group, *Felis,* includes a variety of medium and small wild cats, such as the bobcat, lynx, ocelot, and leopard cat. Also in this group is the species *Felis catus*—all the **domestic,** or tame, cats.

The members of the cat family share many characteristics and habits. All are **carnivorous;** that is, they eat mainly meat. Cats that live in the wild must hunt and kill other animals in order to get their food.

All cats have special body features that help them to hunt **prey** animals successfully. Keen hearing and vision help them to locate animals in tangled forests or among tall grasses. Long, flexible bodies and padded feet allow them to crouch low to the ground and sneak up on their prey. Powerful, muscled legs make cats fast-moving, and sharp teeth make them swift and efficient killers.

Though most domestic cats are fed by their owners and no longer need to hunt for survival, the instincts and physical characteristics of the hunter remain an inborn part of the cat's makeup. Killing mice or birds may seem cruel to humans, but the cat can't change its urge to hunt any more than it can change its whiskers or its tail.

Domestic cats share the hunting instinct of the lion (above), the cheetah (below left), and the leopard (below right).

This African wildcat (left) is probably the direct ancestor of today's domestic cat. The leopard cat (right) is a small modern relative that lives in southern Asia.

Most of today's domestic cats are probably descended from a species of small African wildcat, *Felis libyca.* The ancient Egyptians first tamed these cats many centuries ago to help protect their precious grain from mice. Cats came to be considered sacred animals in Egypt.

Today, cats are popular pets all over the world. Some people raise cats of particular **breeds,** or types. Each breed has its own special characteristics—a particular head or body shape, tail, eye color, and type of coat.

A cat's thick, silky coat, or fur, is often the most striking thing about its appearance. Cats may have long or short hair in a variety of colors—red, brown, black, grey, white, or a combination. The coat of a tabby cat has a pattern of stripes and bars, while a calico cat is marked with large patches of black, red, and cream.

6

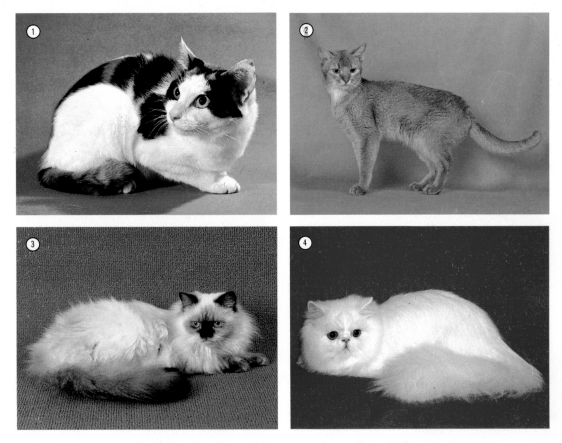

These are 4 of the more than 23 breeds of domestic cats. They fall into two main categories: shorthair and long-hair. In the shorthair group are (1) Japanese calico and (2) Abyssinian. The Siamese cats shown on page 3 represent another well-known breed of shorthair cats. Breeds of long-hair cats include (3) Himalayan and (4) Persian.

A cat's coat protects its skin and insulates its body. It is made up of two types of hair—long, stiff **primary,** or outer, hairs, and softer, shorter **secondary** hairs that form a downy undercoat.

Most cats that people keep as pets are not special breeds but a mixture of several breeds. The two cats shown on the opposite page are such a mixture. The white cat is a female, and the little black cat is her kitten. Let's take a look at the lives of these domestic cats to see how much they have in common with the lives of their wild relatives.

For most of her life, the white cat, like many domestic cats, has spent part of her time indoors, where her owner feeds and cares for her, and part of her time outside, where she hunts mice and roams freely around the neighborhood. During one of the times that she wandered out, she met and mated with a **tomcat** that also lived in the neighborhood. The white female became pregnant. Nine weeks after mating, when the spring flowers were in bloom, she was ready to give birth.

When the time comes for her young to be born, a mother cat's muscles begin to contract in waves to push the babies out of her body. In a few minutes, out comes a kitten, encased in a thin sac of protective membrane. The mother breaks the sac with her tongue and licks the tiny, wet creature clean.

This white female has only one kitten, a black male, but most domestic cats have three to five babies in each **litter.** Wild female cats like lions and leopards usually have litters of about the same size.

The white female licks her newborn kitten.

At birth, the little black cat doesn't look much like the fluffy kittens that people find so attractive. His fur is wet and matted, and his face has a flattened look. The kitten's eyes and ears are sealed shut; he can neither see nor hear. He is very small, weighing only about 3½ ounces (99 grams).

As his mother continues to lick him, the kitten begins to squirm around. The mother cat rolls on her side to expose four pairs of nipples on her stomach and pushes the kitten toward them. Finally he finds a nipple and begins to suck her warm, nourishing milk. His life is off to a good start.

Left: At birth, a kitten's eyes are sealed shut. *Center:* At 10 days, the eyes are beginning to open, but the kitten doesn't have total vision. *Right:* At four weeks, the kitten's eyes and face are completely developed.

For several days to a week after his birth, the kitten stays close to his mother, nursing almost continuously. During this time, he learns to make the milk flow faster by "kneading" the mother's stomach with a pedaling motion of his front paws. His mother's milk will be the kitten's only food for about the first four weeks of his life. His body weight will double in the first week and triple in two weeks. By the time he is four weeks old, the kitten will weigh four times as much as he did when he was born.

The kitten's eyes are cloudy when they first open.

Like domestic kittens, lion cubs can walk when they are about three weeks old.

During these weeks, the kitten is also developing in other ways. His eyes open 8 to 14 days after birth. At first they are cloudy and undeveloped, but they soon become clear. It is not long before tiny teeth begin to develop in his jaws. Eventually the kitten will have 24 to 26 needle-like temporary or baby teeth.

By the age of three weeks, the kitten's eyes and face are fully developed. He is able to walk and eager to explore on his own. Moving on wobbly legs, the kitten touches everything with his sensitive nose and forepaws.

11

At this stage in the kitten's life, the mother cat is very protective. If the kitten gets lost or is frightened, she hears his mewing cries and immediately goes to rescue him and bring him back to her usual resting place. Domestic cats, like lions and other wild cats, carry their young in their mouths by grasping the loose skin on the backs of the youngsters' necks.

When it drinks milk from a dish, a cat curls its tongue up like a spoon.

By the time the kitten is about four weeks old, all his temporary teeth have grown in. Now it is time for him to be **weaned,** or taught to eat food other than his mother's milk. Young domestic cats usually learn to drink milk from a dish and to eat prepared cat foods. After they are weaned, young wild cats eat the small animals that their mother kills and brings to them. Most cats also eat a little grass or some other green plant to aid their digestion.

The kitten's mother teaches him what and how to eat. She also teaches him lifelong habits that are typical of all cats. One habit that the kitten learns very early is that of **grooming,** or washing himself. Both domestic cats and wild cats use their long tongues for this important job.

The surface of a cat's tongue is rough—it feels like sandpaper to the touch. This is because it is covered with tiny hook-like "bristles" called **papillae.** When the cat licks its fur, the tongue brushes out dirt. The licking action also stimulates glands in the skin to produce oils that help to waterproof the fur.

The leopard uses its rough tongue not only for cleaning its fur but also for scraping meat from the bones of prey animals.

The cat's flexible neck allows it to turn and lick almost every part of its body except its head and the area between the shoulder blades. To wash its face and head, the cat licks one of its front paws and rubs it across its head and face over and over again.

Another habit that the kitten learns when he is very young is how to dispose of his body wastes. When the kitten is about two weeks old, his mother carries him outside or to an indoor litter box filled with sand. She teaches him how to dig a hole in the dirt or sand. After eliminating his wastes in the hole, the kitten learns to scrape fresh dirt or sand over the spot with his front paws.

Lion cubs hiding in the grass

By the age of four weeks, the black kitten has become very lively and playful. He seems to have boundless energy and curiosity. The kitten's wild cousins are also full of energy and curiosity at this stage in their lives.

All young cats, whether domestic or wild, are especially attracted to anything that dangles or moves. Dry grass blowing in the wind or a piece of string jerked along the floor will draw their attention and arouse their curiosity. They are alert to any rustling or scratching noises, too. If you scratch your fingers against a rug out of its sight, a kitten will freeze and crouch, staring intently in the direction of the noise.

16

The play of domestic kittens or of other young cats often seems comical to human observers, especially when the youngsters begin chasing their own waving tails. Their play can be amusing, but it has a serious purpose, too. It is part of the learning process that helps young cats to grow into adults.

A dangling mobile makes a fascinating toy.

The black kitten invites his mother to play.

Kittens stalking or pouncing on objects, however clumsy and cute they appear, are displaying inborn hunting behavior. A kitten is "programmed" by instinct to respond to sounds that are like the rustle of prey animals in the grass or to quick movements of any kind.

A cat that spends its life entirely in the house will never actually use these techniques to hunt. It will continue to "play" at stalking and seizing prey. But a cat that is let outside will probably follow its natural instincts and use its skill to find food.

Young cats also practice self-defense skills in their play. If the black kitten had litter mates, he would stage pretend fights with them, pouncing, wrestling, and kicking with his feet. Since he has no brothers or sisters, he tries to get his mother to play with him instead. The kitten signals his wish to play by lying down and rolling on his back or side.

The kitten's invitation to play is just one of the many instinctive body signals that cats use to communicate with each other and with humans.

18

Like people, cats often communicate with sounds. Domestic cats can make more than 60 sounds, from soft mewing to loud screaming, called caterwauling. The low, vibrating sound called **purring** is one that cats use often when they are peaceful and contented. No one knows exactly how a cat makes this unusual sound. It may be caused by vibrations of a blood vessel wall in the cat's chest or of two folds of skin in the cat's throat just behind its vocal cords.

Because lions live in groups, communication is especially important to them.

A lion's roar sends a message that can be heard miles away.

Wild cats also purr and make a variety of other sounds. The lion's roar is one of the most famous means of communication among cats. A lion roars to let both friends and enemies know of its presence.

Domestic cats, like wild cats and many other animals, also communicate by means of odors. A domestic cat has scent glands on its body that produce fluids with an odor that is undetectable by humans. These glands are located on a cat's cheeks and forehead and at the base of its tail. When a friendly cat rubs its head or body against another cat or a human, it is actually marking that animal or person with its own special scent. The cat also puts this scent on objects around its home territory to "claim" that place as its own.

Wild cats mark the boundaries of their territories by the same method.

When a cat is frightened by something, its whole body communicates a message of fear. When the black kitten meets an adult cat other than his mother for the first time (below), he reacts instinctively. He humps his back and arches his tail. All the hairs on his tail and body stand on end. The kitten turns sideways toward the "enemy" and does a kind of stiff-legged strut. All these actions are designed to make the kitten look bigger and more threatening than he really is.

The black kitten meets a strange cat for the first time.

When he ventures outside the house, the kitten meets many new and unfamiliar things. His mother helps him as much as she can, but he must also learn by trial and error how to survive in this strange new world.

The kitten's keen senses of smell, hearing, and touch help him to learn about his surroundings. His sensitive nose picks up food odors and the scents left by other cats and animals that have passed by. A special sense organ in the roof of the kitten's mouth, called **Jacobson's organ,** is also used to detect odors.

The kitten's big, pointed ears pick up a wide range of sounds. A cat's hearing is especially attuned to high-pitched noises like the squeaks of prey animals such as mice. In fact, the kitten can hear many sounds too high or faint for human ears to detect. His ears can turn in the direction of any sounds. Each ear has nearly 30 muscles that allow it to move independently of the other. If you watch your pet cat for a while, you might see one ear suddenly flick to the side, alert to some faraway sound, while the cat's head and other ear remain perfectly still.

The kitten has several ways of staying in touch with his surroundings. On the bottoms of his feet are soft, fleshy pads that are sensitive to touch. The kitten uses his forepaws— the paws on his front feet—almost like hands, touching, grasping, and batting at objects. Some cats even pick up food with a forepaw and put it in their mouths.

With the help of his whiskers, the black kitten can find his way through very narrow openings.

Other important organs of touch are the kitten's whiskers, or **vibrissae**. All cats have long, stiff whiskers above their eyes, around their mouths and noses, and on the insides of their forelegs. When these whiskers touch something, they act like sensitive fingertips, telling the cat that an object is near.

With the help of its whiskers, a cat can learn a great deal about its surroundings. The whiskers around its mouth help a cat to judge the width of an opening it is trying to pass through. Chin whiskers can feel things on the ground below the cat's head, where it can't see. Whiskers on the forelegs are sensitive to the movements of prey between the cat's paws. The "eyebrow" whiskers help to protect a cat's eyes from injury.

24

The mother cat's long mouth whiskers can be seen clearly in this photograph.

As the kitten's senses of touch, hearing, and smell develop, so does his body. A cat's long, strong muscles and flexible joints allow it to move with extraordinary speed and grace. Powerful muscles in the hind legs, combined with a ball-and-socket hip joint, help a cat to climb and to jump easily—sometimes up to 10 feet (3 meters) in one leap. The cat's flexible hip and shoulder joints also allow it to walk on narrow surfaces like tree limbs or the tops of walls.

The black kitten and his distant relative the leopard are both experts at climbing trees.

Cheetahs are the best runners in the cat family. They can reach speeds up to 70 miles (110 kilometers) an hour.

When a cat walks, its front legs swing inward so that both the front leg and the hind leg on one side of its body line up with each other. The cat's legs can actually move in one of several ways, depending on how fast it's going. When walking at a moderate pace, the cat moves both feet on one side of its body at the same time and then the feet on the other side. This is a gait that it shares with only two other animals—the camel and the giraffe.

When it runs, the cat changes its gait to a kind of gallop. It pushes off with both hind legs and comes down first on one foreleg, then the other. Domestic cats can run very fast for short distances—up to 30 miles per hour (48 kilometers per hour) when frightened or escaping from an enemy.

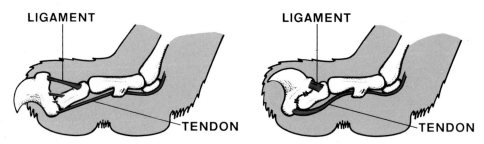

LIGAMENT   LIGAMENT

TENDON   TENDON

Stretchable ligaments and cord-like tendons work to retract or extend a cat's claws. When the tendon is tightened, the claw is extended (left). When the tendon is relaxed, a ligament pulls the claw into a pocket in the cat's paw (right).

Whether walking or running, cats move along on their toes rather than on the bottoms of their feet. All cats have five toes, plus a thumb-like digit called a **dewclaw,** on each front foot. Each hind foot has four toes. All of a cat's toes are equipped with sharp nails, or claws. These hook-like claws serve many purposes, from fighting and catching prey to climbing trees. In all cats except cheetahs, the front claws are **retractile**; that is, they can be pulled back, or retracted, into a pocket in the paw when not in use.

Retractile claws allow cats to walk silently, without the click of claws on the ground. When the claws are retracted, they are also protected from wear and tear. Cats keep their front claws sharp by scratching on trees or pieces of wood. When they do this, they are actually pulling off worn-out layers of protective sheathing that makes the claws dull. To remove the sheathing from their hind claws, they chew it off with their teeth. Cats that live indoors may scratch their claws on furniture. Often they can be trained to use a special scratching post instead.

In addition to claws, the cat's most important weapons for hunting and self-defense are its teeth. By the age of five or six months, the black kitten's baby teeth will be replaced by 30 adult teeth. Adult cats have 2 pairs of sharp, fanglike **canine** teeth; 12 small **incisors,** 6 between each pair of canines; and 14 **molars** behind the canines.

The canine teeth bite, the incisors scrape, and the molars cut. Unlike human molars, which are flat teeth used for grinding food, the cat's molars are pointed. Cats don't chew their food. Instead, they cut it into pieces small enough to digest, using a scissors-like movement of their molars. When a cat eats, it tips its head sideways to position the food between its molars for cutting.

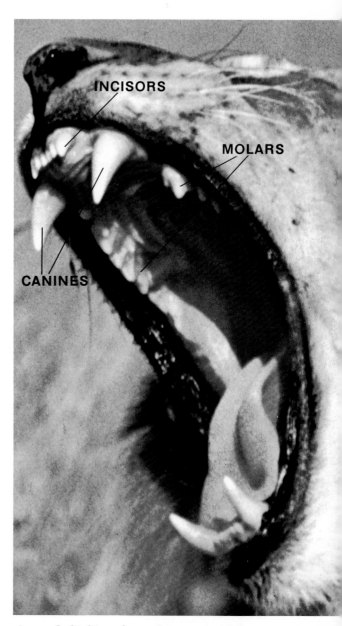

An adult lion has the same 30 teeth as an adult domestic cat.

Walking along a narrow tree branch is one of the many outdoor skills that the black kitten has learned.

By the time the kitten is three or four months old, he has spent many hours outdoors with his mother, learning hunting techniques and the ways of the world outside the house. At first he needed her protection all the time. But now his body has grown rapidly. Although he has not reached full maturity, he has many of the skills and the physical strength he needs to take care of himself.

Now that her kitten is a young cat, the mother begins to separate herself from him. Many wild animals go through this process. As soon as their offspring are able to take care of themselves, the parents drive them away. Though it may seem heartless to human observers, this behavior is necessary for the survival of the species.

Most wild cats, except for lions, are loners. Their hunting techniques are suited to hunting and living alone rather than in groups or packs. Young cats must go off alone to find their own hunting territory. If they remained in their parents' territory, there wouldn't be enough prey in the area to go around. Also, a mother that became pregnant again and had

new babies to care for would be unable to take care of her older offspring.

Although these exact conditions don't apply to domestic cats, separation from the mother is another of the wild traits that lingers on as an instinct in many domestic cats. It is this heritage of a solitary life that gives cats such an independent nature. Though they like companionship at certain times, they also spend a lot of time roaming around alone.

To start the young cat off on his own, the mother cat hisses and swipes her paw at him when he tries to approach her. After a few more attempts to get near her, he learns to go his own way.

Crayfish (right) and gold-fish in a pond (above) are some of the animals that the young cat meets in his wanderings.

The young cat is now about four months old. As the weeks go by, he learns a solitary and independent way of life. Before separating from his mother, he spent an average of three or four hours a day outdoors. Now, he spends more and more time outside—up to six or eight hours a day.

During his wanderings, he investigates anything that moves, watching intently and touching with a tentative paw. He sometimes encounters creatures like crayfish and pet goldfish that are not the usual cat prey, and he merely plays with them. But he also practices his stalking techniques, waiting motionless for long periods of time in the grass and watching for likely prey.

Sometimes he sleeps, taking the endless series of "cat naps" that occupy nearly two-thirds of the average cat's life.

34

When they are not exploring or lying in wait for prey, young lions and domestic cats spend much of their time dozing in the sun.

As the black cat grows, he begins to go out more and more during the night, when many prey animals are abroad. His eyesight is specially adapted to help him see well at night.

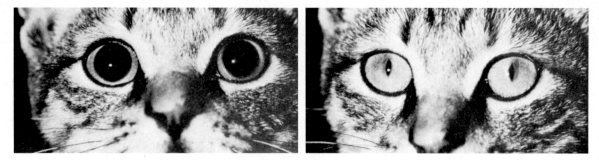

In dim light, a cat's pupils expand to let in as much light as possible (left). When the light is bright, the pupils contract to small slits (right).

Like human eyes, a cat's eye has an opening in the center, the pupil, through which light passes. Muscles in the iris, the colored part of the eye, work to expand the pupil when it's dark outside so that all available light can get in. Because its pupils are extra large, a cat can see quite well in dim light, although of course it can't see in total darkness.

A cat also has a special layer of cells behind its eyes, called the **tapetum lucidum,** that acts like a mirror to reflect additional light into the eyes. This reflection produces the eerie "night shine" that you see in a cat's eyes after dark.

A cat's eye is protected by two furry eyelids and by an additional third eyelid, the **nictitating membrane,** at the eye's inner corner. This special eyelid is partly transparent and helps to lubricate and shield the eye.

The cat depends on its excellent vision in spotting and seizing prey. Cats, like humans, see a three-dimensional picture when they look at the world. Each eye sees a slightly different view, and the two fields of vision overlap to give a cat the ability to judge depth and distance.

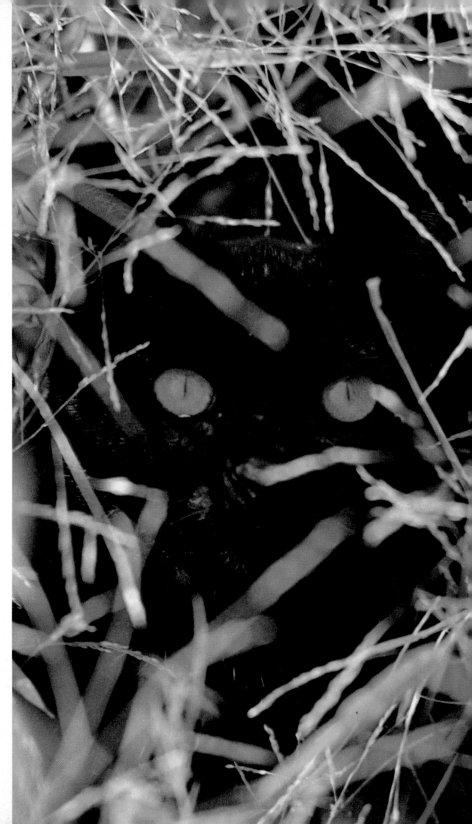

The pupils of a domestic cat are vertical in shape. Lions, tigers, and some other wild cats have round pupils.

38

The black cat catches his first mouse.

Using his special night vision and his long-practiced hunting skills, the young cat finally catches and kills his first
mouse. First he stalks the mouse. He may have to wait,
nearly motionless, for hours outside the mouse's hiding place
until the mouse shows itself. Once he spots the mouse, he
creeps up on it silently. He crouches and lies in wait, judging
the exact distance between himself and the mouse. When
he's close enough, he pounces, lightning quick. He springs
forward and grabs the mouse, claws extended. When spring-
ing, he stays low to the ground. He doesn't actually leap
up but keeps his hind feet firmly planted on the ground
for balance.

Once the mouse is in his grasp, he delivers a quick killing
bite at the neck with his canine teeth. The mouse dies
instantly, and the cat carries off his trophy. If he is hungry,
he may eat his catch. If not, he will probably take the
mouse home, planning to save it for a future meal.

Now that the once-tiny kitten is almost a full-fledged adult tomcat, he begins to stake out his own hunting territory. Although both male and female cats mark territory for themselves, the tomcat usually has a wider range than the female.

Most house cats will defend the yard area around the house as their exclusive territory. If an outsider approaches, the cat displays anger by laying back its ears and bristling all over. It gives the offender a threatening stare and may hiss, spit, and growl, its tail switching back and forth warningly. Usually the intruder backs off without a fight. Sometimes two cats fight it out, but this is rare.

The black tomcat has marked his territory well by scratching on the surrounding trees and by spraying scent and strong-smelling urine on bushes and objects around and in his territory. This warns other cats not to trespass.

Two unfriendly cats exchange threats as night begins to fall.

Domestic cats also have a wider "home range"—a territory sometimes many acres in size—that they patrol regularly but share with other neighborhood cats. Sometimes, especially at night, several cats will meet in this area and lie down close to one another in live-and-let-live companionship.

By wintertime, the little black kitten that was born in the spring is nearly full grown. As an adult, he may be 8 to 10 inches (20-25 centimeters) tall at the shoulder and may weigh 6 to 15 pounds (2.7-7 kilograms), although some big tomcats have been known to reach weights of 20 pounds (9 kilograms) or more. The cat can be expected to live for 8 to 20 (or, in rare cases, 30) years, depending on luck and on the care he receives from his owner.

At 7 to 10 months, the black cat will be able to father kittens himself. Perhaps his owner will choose to have him **neutered** so that he cannot reproduce. Females can also be neutered to keep them from having litters. This routine operation, done by a veterinarian, does not, as many people think, make cats act strange or lazy. Rather, it helps to keep down the overpopulation that results in so many homeless and unwanted cats left to wander city streets and alleys.

When the first snow of winter falls, the black cat hesitates at the door of the house. He touches the snow cautiously with his paw and finally ventures out. This cold white world is unfamiliar to him, but he is not afraid. With his curious and independent nature, he will soon be as much at home in the snow-covered streets as he was among the bright flowers of summer.

GLOSSARY

breed—a type of cat with its own special characteristics, which distinguish it from other types of cats

canine (KAY-nine) teeth—sharp, pointed teeth used for biting

carnivorous (kar-NIV-or-ous)—meat-eating

dewclaw—a thumb-like toe on a cat's front paw

domestic—tame; domestic animals depend on humans for food and care.

grooming—the act of washing and cleaning the fur

incisor (in-SI-zuhr) teeth—pointed teeth used for scraping

Jacobson's organ—a special organ in the roof of a cat's mouth that combines the senses of smell and taste

litter—the offspring born to a mother cat at one time

molar teeth—a cat's back teeth, designed for cutting

neutered (NEWT-uhrd)—made unable to reproduce by means of an operation that removes reproductive organs

nictitating (NIK-teh-tate-ing) membrane—a third eyelid located at the inner corner of a cat's eye

papillae (puh-PIL-ee)—tiny hook-like projections on a cat's tongue

prey—an animal that is hunted and killed by another animal for food

primary hairs—the long, stiff hairs of a cat's outer coat

46

purring—the low, vibrating sound made by a contented cat

retractile (ree-TRAK-t'l) claws—claws that can be pulled in

secondary hairs—the soft, downy hairs of a cat's undercoat

tapetum lucidum (teh-PEET-uhm LU-sehd-um)—a layer of cells in a cat's eye that acts like a mirror to reflect light into the eye

tomcat—an adult male cat

vibrissae (vih-BRIS-ee)—hairs or whiskers that are sensitive to touch

weaned—able to take food other than mother's milk

INDEX